The Nursery Rhymes of
Winnie the Pooh

A Classic Disney Treasury

Ladybird

A Catalogue record for this book is available from the British Library.

Published by Ladybird Books Ltd
27 Wrights Lane
LONDON
W8 5TZ

A Penguin Company

2 4 6 8 10 9 7 5 3 1

Ladybird and the device of a Ladybird are trademarks of Ladybird Books Ltd.

http://www.ladybird.co.uk

Printed in Spain

Table of Contents

The Nursery Rhymes of
Winnie the Pooh

A-Hunting We Will Go

A-hunting we will go,
A-hunting we will go.
Hi, ho, the merry-o,
A-hunting we will go.

Frere Jacques

Frere Jacques, Frere Jacques,

Dormez-vous? Dormez-vous?

Sonnez les matines,

Sonnez les matines.

Ding, dang, dong,

Ding, dang, dong.

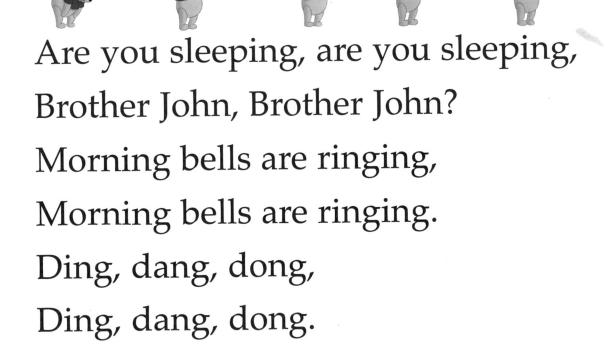

Are you sleeping, are you sleeping,

Brother John, Brother John?

Morning bells are ringing,

Morning bells are ringing.

Ding, dang, dong,

Ding, dang, dong.

Baa, Baa, Black Sheep

Baa, baa, black sheep, have you any wool?

Yes sir, yes sir, three bags full;

One for the master, and one for the dame,

And one for the little boy who lives down the lane.

Bye, Baby Bunting

Bye, baby bunting,

Daddy's gone a-hunting,

Gone to get a rabbit skin

To wrap the baby bunting in.

Clap, Clap, Clap Your Hands

Clap, clap, clap your hands,

Clap your hands together.

Clap, clap, clap your hands,

Clap your hands right now.

Did You Ever See a Laddie?

Did you ever see a laddie,

A laddie, a laddie?

Did you ever see a laddie

Go this way and that?

Go this way and that way,

Go this way and that way.

Did you ever see a laddie

Go this way and that?

15

The Farmer in the Dell

The farmer in the dell, the farmer in the dell,

Hi, ho, the derry-o, the farmer in the dell.

The farmer takes a wife, the farmer takes a wife,

Hi, ho, the derry-o, the farmer takes a wife.

The wife takes a child, the wife takes a child,

Hi, ho, the derry-o, the wife takes a child.

The child takes a nurse, the child takes a nurse,

Hi, ho, the derry-o, the child takes a nurse.

The nurse takes a dog, the nurse takes a dog,

Hi, ho, the derry-o, the nurse takes a dog.

The dog takes a cat, the dog takes a cat,

Hi, ho, the derry-o, the dog takes a cat.

The cat takes a mouse, the cat takes a mouse,

Hi, ho, the derry-o, the cat takes a mouse.

The mouse takes the cheese, the mouse takes the cheese,

Hi, ho, the derry-o, the mouse takes the cheese.

The cheese stands alone, the cheese stands alone,

Hi, ho, the derry-o, the cheese stands alone.

Head and Shoulders, Knees and Toes

Head and shoulders, knees and toes, knees and toes,

Head and shoulders, knees and toes, knees and toes.

Eyes and ears and mouth and nose,

Head and shoulders, knees and toes, knees and toes.

Here We Go 'Round the Mulberry Bush

Here we go 'round the mulberry bush,

The mulberry bush, the mulberry bush.

Here we go 'round the mulberry bush,

So early in the morning.

Hey Diddle Diddle

Hey diddle diddle,

The cat and the fiddle,

The cow jumped over the moon.

The little dog laughed to see such sport,

And the dish ran away with the spoon.

Hickory, Dickory, Dock

Hickory, dickory, dock!

The mouse ran up the clock.

The clock struck one,

The mouse ran down,

Hickory, dickory, dock!

26

Hush, Little Baby

Hush, little baby, don't say a word,
Mama's gonna buy you a mocking bird.
If that mocking bird won't sing,
Mama's gonna buy you a diamond ring.

If that diamond ring turns brass,

Mama's gonna buy you a looking glass.

If that looking glass gets broke,

Mama's gonna buy you a billy goat.

If that billy goat won't pull,

Mama's gonna buy you a cart and bull.

If that cart and bull turn over,

Mama's gonna buy you a dog named Rover.

If that dog named Rover won't bark,

Mama's gonna buy you a horse and cart.

If that horse and cart fall down,

You'll still be the sweetest little baby in town.

Doctor Foster

Doctor Foster went to Gloucester,

In a shower of rain.

He stepped in a puddle

Right up to his middle,

And never went there again.

I'm a Little Teapot

I'm a little teapot, short and stout,
Here's my handle, here's my spout.
When the water's boiling, hear me shout,
"Tip me up and pour me out!"

If You're Happy and You Know It

If you're happy and you know it,
clap your hands.

Clap, clap.

If you're happy and you know it,
clap your hands.

Clap, clap.

If you're happy and you know it,
And you really want to show it,
If you're happy and you know it,
clap your hands.

Clap, clap.

If you're happy and you know it,
stamp your feet.

Stamp, stamp.

If you're happy and you know it,
stamp your feet.

Stamp, stamp.

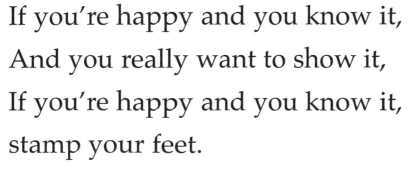

If you're happy and you know it,
And you really want to show it,
If you're happy and you know it,
stamp your feet.

Stamp, stamp.

35

If you're happy and you know it,
nod your head.

Nod, nod.

If you're happy and you know it,
nod your head.

Nod, nod.

If you're happy and you know it,
And you really want to show it,
If you're happy and you know it,
nod your head.

Nod, nod.

If you're happy and you know it,
pat your knees.

Pat, pat.

If you're happy and you know it,
pat your knees.

Pat, pat.

If you're happy and you know it,
And you really want to show it,
If you're happy and you know it,
pat your knees.

Pat, pat.

Humpty Dumpty

Humpty Dumpty sat on a wall,
Humpty Dumpty had a great fall.
All the King's horses,
And all the King's men,
Couldn't put Humpty together again.

It's Raining, It's Pouring

It's raining, it's pouring,

The old man is snoring.

He went to bed

And bumped his head,

And couldn't get up in the morning.

Incey Wincey Spider

Incey wincey spider climbing up the spout,

40

Down came the rain
and washed the spider out.

Out came the sunshine,
dried up all the rain.
Incey wincey spider
climbing up again.

Jack and Jill

Jack and Jill went up the hill

To fetch a pail of water.

Jack fell down and broke his crown,

And Jill came tumbling after.

Jack Be Nimble

Jack be nimble,

Jack be quick,

Jack jump over the candlestick.

Ladybird, Ladybird

Ladybird, ladybird, fly away home,
Your house is on fire, your children are gone;
All except one, and her name is Ann,
And she has crept under the frying pan.

Lazy Mary

Lazy Mary, will you get up,

Will you get up,

Will you get up?

Lazy Mary, will you get up,

Will you get up this morning?

Little Duckie Duddle

Little Duckie Duddle

Went wading in a puddle,

Went wading in a puddle quite small.

Said he, "It doesn't matter

How much I splash and splatter,

I'm only a duckie, after all. *Quack, quack.*"

Little Green Frog

Ah - ump, went the little green frog one day.

Ah - ump, went the little green frog.

Ah - ump, went the little green frog one day.

And his green eyes went *blink, blink, blink.*

Little Jack Horner

Little Jack Horner sat in a corner,

Eating his Christmas pie.

He put in his thumb and pulled out a plum,

And said, "What a good boy am I!"

London Bridge

London Bridge is falling down, falling down,
   falling down,
London Bridge is falling down, my fair lady.
Take the key and lock him up, lock him up,
   lock him up,
Take the key and lock him up, my fair lady.

Mary Had a Little Lamb

Mary had a little lamb,

Its fleece was white as snow,

And everywhere that Mary went

The lamb was sure to go.

It followed her to school one day,

Which was against the rule.

It made the children laugh and play

To see a lamb at school.

And so the teacher turned it out,

But still it lingered near,

And waited patiently about

Till Mary did appear.

"Why does the lamb love Mary so?"

The eager children cry.

"Why, Mary loves the lamb, you know,"

The teacher did reply.

Mary, Mary, Quite Contrary

Mary, Mary, quite contrary,

How does your garden grow?

"With silver bells and cockle shells

And pretty maids all in a row."

I Had a Little Nut Tree

I had a little nut tree
  Nothing would it bear
But a silver nutmeg
  And a golden pear.

The King of Spain's daughter
  Came to visit me,
And all for the sake
  Of my little nut tree.

Miss Polly Had a Dolly

Miss Polly had a dolly who was
    sick, sick, sick,
So she phoned for the doctor to come
    quick, quick, quick.
The doctor came with his bag and his hat,
And he rapped at the door with a
    rat-tat-tat.
He looked at the dolly and he shook his head,
And he said, "Miss Polly, put her straight to bed."
He wrote on a paper for a
    pill, pill, pill,
"I'll be back tomorrow with my
    bill, bill, bill!"

58

The Muffin Man

Do you know the muffin man,
　the muffin man,
　the muffin man?
Do you know the muffin man,
　who lives in Drury Lane?

Yes I know the muffin man,
　the muffin man,
　the muffin man.
Yes I know the muffin man,
　who lives in Drury Lane.

Oats and Beans and Barley Grow

Oats and beans and
barley grow,
Oats and beans and
barley grow.

But not you nor I nor anyone knows
How oats and beans and barley grow.

Old King Cole

Old King Cole was a merry old soul,

And a merry old soul was he.

He called for his pipe and he called for his bowl,

And he called for his fiddlers three.

Old Macdonald

Old Macdonald had a farm,
    E-I-E-I-O.
And on that farm he had a pig,
    E-I-E-I-O.
With an oink oink here,
And an oink oink there,
Here an oink, there an oink,
Everywhere an oink oink.
Old Macdonald had a farm,
    E-I-E-I-O.

62

Tom the Piper's Son

Tom he was a piper's son,

He learned to play when he was young,

But the only tune that he could play,

Was 'Over the Hills and Far Away.'

Now Tom with his pipe

did play with such skill,

That those who heard him

could never keep still.

Pat-a-Cake

Pat-a-cake, pat-a-cake, baker's man,

Bake me a cake as fast as you can.

Pat it and roll it and mark it with B,

And put it in the oven for baby and me.

Pease Porridge Hot

Pease porridge hot, pease porridge cold,
Pease porridge in the pot, nine days old.

Some like it hot, some like it cold,
Some like it in the pot, nine days old.

Pop Goes the Weasel

Half a pound of tuppeny rice,

Half a pound of treacle,

Mix it up and make it nice,

Pop! goes the weasel.

Ring-a-Ring o' Roses

Ring-a-ring o' roses,

A pocket full of posies.

A-tishoo! A-tishoo!

We all fall down!

Hush-a-Bye, Baby

Hush-a-bye, baby, on the tree top,

When the wind blows, the cradle will rock.

When the bough breaks, the cradle will fall,
And down will come baby, cradle and all.

71

Row, Row, Row Your Boat

Row, row, row your boat

Gently down the stream.

Merrily, merrily, merrily, merrily,

Life is but a dream.

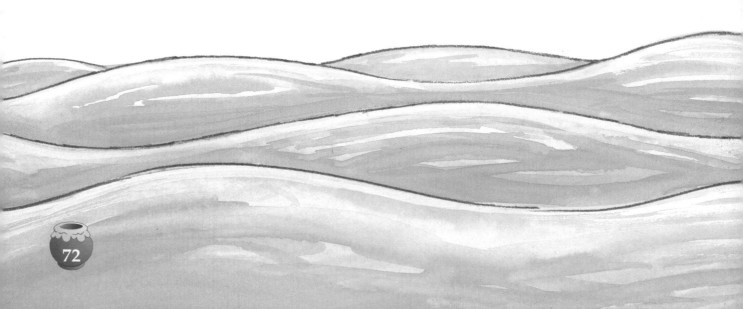

Rub-a-dub-dub

Rub-a-dub-dub, three men in a tub,

And who do you think they be?

The butcher, the baker,

   the candlestick maker.

Turn them out, knaves all three.

See-Saw, Margery Daw

See-saw, Margery Daw,
Johnny shall have a new master.
He shall have but a penny a day,
because he can't work any faster.

Shoe the Horse

Shoe the horse, shoe the horse,

Shoe the bay mare.

Here a nail, there a nail,

Still she stands there.

Sing a Song of Sixpence

Sing a song of sixpence, a pocket full of rye.

Four and twenty blackbirds baked in a pie.

When the pie was opened,

　　the birds began to sing.

Wasn't that a dainty dish to set before the king?

Swing Our Hands

Swing our hands, swing our hands,
swing our hands together.

Swing our hands, swing our hands,
in our circle now.
Tap our toes, tap our toes,
tap our toes together.
Tap our toes, tap our toes,
in our circle now.

Teddy Bear

Teddy bear, teddy bear, turn around,

Teddy bear, teddy bear, touch the ground.

Teddy bear, teddy bear, turn out the light,

Teddy bear, teddy bear, say good night.

Grand Old Duke of York

Oh, the grand old Duke of York,

He had ten thousand men.

He marched them up to the top of the hill,

And he marched them down again.

And when they were up, they were up.

And when they were down, they were down.

And when they were only halfway up,

They were neither up nor down.

This Is the Way We Wash Our Clothes

This is the way we wash our clothes,

    wash our clothes, wash our clothes.

82

This is the way we wash our clothes,

so early in the morning.

This Little Pig

This little pig went to market,

This little pig stayed home.

This little pig had roast beef,

This little pig had none.

And this little pig cried,

Wee, wee, wee, all the way home.

Twinkle, Twinkle, Little Star

Twinkle, twinkle, little star,

How I wonder what you are.

Up above the world so high,

Like a diamond in the sky.

Twinkle, twinkle, little star,

How I wonder what you are.

The Wheels on the Bus

The wheels on the bus go round and round,
round and round, round and round.
The wheels on the bus go round and round,
all day long.
The baby on the bus goes wah wah wah,
wah wah wah, wah wah wah,
The baby on the bus goes wah wah wah,
all day long.
The lights on the bus go blink blink blink,
blink blink blink, blink blink blink,
The lights on the bus go blink blink blink,
all day long.

The driver on the bus says, "Move to the back, move to the back, move to the back, move to the back."
The driver on the bus says, "Move to the back,"
  all day long.

The money on the bus goes clink clink clink,
  clink clink clink, clink clink clink,
The money on the bus goes, clink clink clink,
  all day long.

The people on the bus go up and down,
up and down, up and down,
The people on the bus go up and down,
all day long.

The wipers on the bus go, swish swish swish,
swish swish swish, swish swish swish,
The wipers on the bus go, swish swish swish,
all day long.

Where Is Thumbkin?

Where is Thumbkin?

Where is Thumbkin?

Here I am, here I am.

How are you today, sir?

Very well, I thank you.

Run away, run away.

92

Little Miss Muffet

Little Miss Muffet
    Sat on her tuffet,
Eating her curds and whey.
    Along came a spider
That sat down beside her,
    And frightened Miss Muffet away.

Yankee Doodle

Yankee Doodle came to town,
    riding on a pony;
He stuck a feather in his cap
    and called it macaroni.
Yankee Doodle keep it up,
    Yankee Doodle Dandy.
Mind the music and the step,
    and with the girls be handy.